From the time I was born, my mother always made sure I felt secure in life. Yes, times have been tough, but we've gotten through everything together. With every obstacle, there's been a lesson learned. She has taught me how to get through life and stay strong. I couldn't ask God for a better mom. This book is an authentic representation of who my mom is and what we've gone through. I hope it encourages all of the moms who read it and reminds them that they're not alone.

—*Jaslyn Edgar, Nikki's daughter*

This is a life-changing book for single moms. It is so hard juggling life, kids, and your own heart when you are single. So often we overlook ourselves in the process of taking care of everyone else. So take time to enjoy this thirty-one-day process of finding yourself and your purpose.

—*Kimberly Jones Pothier, author of* Beautifully Whole

Every single mother feels like a ship alone at sea at times. Single mothers have become the modern-day widow, and the percentage rises every year. To be seen and to know they are not alone is a rare gift to any mother. Regardless how a woman finds herself in the role of single parenting, to feel she is not alone and can raise exceptional humans is all the encouragement she sometimes needs. Nikki offers encouragement and hope that all is not lost, and that heroes sometimes look like women who are both mother and father to their kids.

—*Rita Springer, songwriter, singer, leader*

All Things Beautiful

31 Devotions for Single Moms

Nikki Leonti Edgar

BroadStreet
PUBLISHING

BroadStreet Publishing® Group, LLC
Savage, Minnesota, USA
BroadStreetPublishing.com

All Things Beautiful: 31 Devotions for Single Moms

ISBN-13: 978-1-4245-5628-1 (hardcover)
ISBN-13: 978-1-4245-5629-8 (e-book)

Stock or custom editions of BroadStreet Publishing titles may be purchased in bulk for educational, business, ministry, fundraising, or sales promotional use. For information, please email info@broadstreetpublishing.com.

Cover design by Chris Garborg at garborgdesign.com
Interior design and typesetting by Katherine Lloyd at theDESKonline.com

Printed in China
18 19 20 21 22 5 4 3 2 1

＊

This book is dedicated to the beautiful girl
who made me a mommy. The greatest decision
of my life was you. Thank you for watching me grow up
and having patience while I learned what it means to be
a parent. You made it through my time as a teenager, and I
made it through your time as a teenager. Jaslyn, thank you.
From the deepest parts of my heart, I love you.

Contents

Foreword

by Holly Wagner

*O*ver the last few years, I have spent quite a bit of time with Nikki Edgar. During casual dinners, she will occasionally belt out a song, which is inspiring and annoying at the same time! Her voice is just beyond belief, especially to someone like me who can't sing two notes in the same key. She is just one of those people you want to hang around— not because she is perfect and has it all together, but because she is real. With Nikki, you know you can have a genuine conversation and find an authentic friend.

I have watched her walk through some tough situations, and I have seen her stay faithful to the God who loves her. She is refreshingly honest, and in Los Angeles, which can be the city of 'fake,' that is such a treasure.

Being a mom is a hard job, and I can only imagine the challenges that come with being a single mom. In all seasons, Nikki has handled her role as mom with inspiring grace.

As I read through her book, *All Things Beautiful*, I experienced a lot of different emotions and was honestly encouraged to trust God more. I am not a single mom, but I was refreshed with each chapter.

I love this girl, and I know that you will too. You will feel like you are having a conversation with a friend. And if you want to hear her sing and you can't make it to dinner, you should check out her music on iTunes. You will see what I mean about her amazing voice!

Holly Wagner
Pastor, Oasis Church, Los Angeles, CA
Author, *Find Your Brave*

1

Dream Catching

Maybe you've heard it said that writing out your dreams and goals is not only cathartic, but it also helps increase your faith and gives you an opportunity to see what God can do. I write out a list of my goals for the year every January first, but you can start this at any time. On these lists would be my intentions, dreams, desires, or even things I considered to be a little foolish. Some years, my list would start with braces for my daughter and end with writing my own book. (Hey, hey! I'm doing that now.)

I make a list of prayers for my family, and I used to make a list when asking God for a spouse. I wrote out everything that was important to me in a partner and what was an absolute in character. From loving my children to loving God, I carefully listed around twenty things that were non-negotiable. A year after I made this list, God sent me someone who was exactly what I prayed for. Down to every single detail.

Writing down our desires and prayers also serves as a constant reminder of what we deserve and what we should set out to attain. If I met a guy that I kept making excuses for, or if I thought I could let a couple of things slip just because I was attracted to someone, I would pull out my list and remind myself that my prayer was for someone who was truthful, caring, patient, etc. Like it did for me, a list can help you maintain focus and set a clear vision of the overall goal.

You can also take the things you pray for in a mate and turn them around on yourself. If my list was for someone honest, kind, open-hearted, nonjudgmental, and focused, I would then ask God to help me lead with kindness, honesty, and an open heart. You attract the things that are overflowing from within you. This goes for relationships, work, and other areas of life.

In 2012, I made a list as I do every year. I asked the Lord for a nice apartment for myself and my kids, a new job, and an island in my kitchen. God definitely has a sense of humor, because when it came time for me to find a new place to live, at the end of the walk-through, the owner showed me an old island cart that he said I could use for the kitchen. It wasn't the vision I had in my mind, but it sure was a detail of my prayer that didn't get overlooked. To this day, it makes me giggle when I think about that little wheeled island that I would make cookies on while I thanked God that I had worked my way out of sleeping on couches or counting quarters.

I encourage you to take a couple of minutes and journal some of your prayers and desires. Don't be conservative with your dreams; really go all the way. Watch what God can do and how seeing these things in front of you will stir a motivation within you to take steps toward your destiny.

Invite God into every aspect of your life and he will direct and bless you. He cares about the desires of your heart and will weave your dreams together beautifully.

In all your ways acknowledge him, and he will make straight your paths.

PROVERBS 3:6 ESV

Lord, I acknowledge you today and ask for you to open the windows of my heart so that I can clearly see your paths. I invite you into every situation of my life. Thank you for your goodness and care in all the details.

What are some dreams that you have
for this year?

2

When You Just Want to Move On ... But You Can't

ell, let's face it. I didn't always make the best decisions. I settled for things I knew weren't the best for me, I made a ton of excuses, and I didn't listen to other people's opinions. As an eighteen-year-old newly married woman, I thought I knew it all. I look back and laugh as I now look at my seventeen-year-old daughter and can't imagine her being a married mom like I was. And to think that I thought I had it all together!

By the time I walked through a second divorce (yes, second), I was finally ready to surrender to God and move on. Unfortunately, as you probably know, even though you're ready to move on to new things, your past has a way of sticking around. Whether it be in the voice of a mother-in-law, calls from your ex-husband about school details, or old unpaid bills, the past has a way of reminding us where we went wrong. It may seem like you'll never escape the reminders that you didn't always make the best choices, but I promise you'll overcome.

The headaches of your past can creep in whether the other parent is in the picture or not. I thought my divorce would bring finality, but for me it was the beginning of a very long road. From continuous custody battles to meddling family members, I felt like the light would never shine through the tunnel.

Can I say right now that I'm completely on the other side? Well ... no. My older two children are teens and things are easier, but I still have to face reminders like the ghosts of Christmas in the *Scrooge* movie. They can lead me back through the darkest corners of my life where I can't believe I'd ever ventured. I constantly remind myself that God has not failed me and that I have made it through 100 percent of the battles I've faced. One hundred percent is great odds that I'll make it out of what I'm going through right now too.

You may be reading this wondering how you'll endure another day of friction, worry, or upset. But if you continue to look to the one who will never fail you, I promise he will keep you above the circumstances that are trying to hold you captive in negativity. The turmoil may not become easier overnight—in many cases it won't—but your faith in the knowledge that you will overcome and that there will be restoration in your story will be the wings to guide you through the uncertainty of your life.

Let the spirit of God who dwells in your heart and mind move you forward and above when the arms of your past want to drag you back down.

Beauty Mark

Let the beauty and grace from within you shine through the darkness that may be surrounding you. You can ignite a difference in your life and in those around you.

From the end of the earth will I cry unto thee, when my heart is overwhelmed: lead me to the rock that is higher than I.
PSALM 61:2 KJV

Lord, I ask for patience to handle the things that overwhelm my mind. Help me be slow to anger but rich in grace and understanding. Fill me with your love so it may overflow to my children and those around me.

What things are overwhelming you?
Write down the name of someone who
can support you in that area.

Journal

3

When Your Life
Is Flipped

ell, if you've ever been involved in a home restoration
project or watched one of the many house-flipping
TV shows, you know there's a lot more to it than what you
see in the thirty minutes that they neatly wrap into one
very gratifying program. A renovation can bring leaks, broken pipes, permits, paperwork, termites, and other random
curveballs. If you were to start a home project without any
knowledge of the in-between, you'd probably be seriously
disappointed that it's not as glamorous as it appears.

As children and teenagers, we have ideals and dreams of
what we think our life is going to look like. My dreams were
so detailed that anything less would've been deemed failure
in my eyes. With my purity ring on my finger, I imagined
kissing my future spouse for the first time when he proposed
to me, losing my virginity on our wedding night, having our

first child five years after our wedding and our second child two years after that. We would live in an old home that we restored together and life would be complete bliss.

I was a dreamer and a romantic comedy addict. When my life started to look different from that, I began to feel like a failure and believed that I would never have the happy ending I visualized. I saw the before and after of my life but didn't grasp the in-between. I put my future in a neat little presentation with the big red bow. I saw the house with the beautiful shiplap, original hardwood floors, and of course the *wow* moment, but I had no idea of the journey it would take to get there.

Oh, but the life we live to get to the beauty isn't always beautiful, and it definitely doesn't happen in thirty minutes. There's pain in the process of refining.

Like myself, you may have ventured far away from your original dream. This doesn't mean you can't have a beautiful story. A detour is only a side road on the way to your destiny. You can't perfectly plan your life and not expect to have some bumps along the way. You also can't live in a mindset where you believe you have already failed because things didn't go the way you imagined them.

You may be in over your head with something you didn't imagine would be this difficult, or you may be losing hope that you'll have the extraordinary life you imagined. I can tell you with certainty that no matter how many things may be going wrong in your house, you're on a path to something beautiful. It may look like the biggest mess you've ever seen, but there is a restoration process that is going to lead you to something better than you could've ever imagined.

Give God the uncertainties and difficulties of your situation. Have faith that he can guide you through the steps of unveiling your restored dreams.

And I will restore to you the years that the locust hath eaten.
JOEL 2:25 KJV

Lord, I ask you to fill my heart with renewed hope. You are a God who restores the broken with your redeeming love. Reignite my dreams and help me see that beauty can arise from any circumstance.

What is one life project that is
in the process of healing for you?

4

Money Doesn't Make the World Go 'Round, But It Gives It a Nice Push

can't tell you how many almost head-on collisions I've had with my purse. It wasn't easy and it sure wasn't pretty. One of the areas in my life where it's actually been easier for me to have faith is my finances. I was always confident that if I believed in God's provision and stayed generous to others, he wouldn't let me down. Let me tell you, he never has. There have been some near misses, but he has always come through even if it was on the very last day.

Kids cost money. I've heard it said that they are "just another plate on the table," but they're so much more than that—especially if they want to do sports, cheer, and vocal lessons. The costs of activities all add up and can be a strain on a single parent.

Now the truth is, at times my life was a giant chaotic mess. At one point in my single-mom journey, I spent several months sleeping with my kids on my brother's couch. My brother and sister-in-law already had two kids of their own and a couple of other people living in their home. Those few months were difficult but also joyful. I didn't have to worry about paying rent, gas, water, or electricity. A local church had a single-moms' ministry that gave me a car free and clear. The fifty dollars a week I made singing worship at a local church paid for my groceries. I was at the beginning of rediscovering my dreams and knew this wouldn't last forever.

I decided to find joy in that moment. As cramped and void of privacy as it was, I used it as an opportunity to let go and trust wholeheartedly that God had a plan for my life that I had not even seen yet. Slowly but surely he brought new opportunities my way that would eventually get me back on my feet and into my own place.

My older daughter's birth father never contributed but a couple of checks for child support. He hadn't seen her in over ten years when my now-husband adopted her. I was the sole provider for her and was the provider for my son, for whom I was sending a check to his father every month. The financial extremes I was living in made absolutely no sense. I was also responsible for paying for all the flights to visit my son, car rentals, and hotel rooms, not to mention taking time off work. I thought I would never get ahead. How could

I get a place when I was paying so much for child support and expenses?

Even so, God showed me endless miracles. I was on a flight and got bumped off. I showed kindness to the airline employee and was given $2,000 in vouchers. This paid for five months of trips to Florida. I was constantly left in tears at the miraculous ways God made sure I didn't sink.

Living with eleven people wasn't my view of a miracle at the time. However, it was God's miracle to afford me the opportunity to do what I needed to do to inevitably be where he wanted me to be. If you can rest your heart in his hands and truly trust that he is making a way for you in this very moment, I know you will be one step closer to freedom in whatever financial situation you're in.

There is no debt too large and no paper trail too long that he can't make a miracle in your finances. I had a *zero* credit score, debt with the IRS, a home foreclosure, three car repossessions, and broken leases—not to mention personal debts and the need to pawn every nice piece of jewelry I owned. My home storage was robbed in between moves, and I had to start all over with only suitcases to my name. Still, there isn't a detail that he hasn't covered. Everything that has ever been stolen from me the Lord has given back. I cried out to him so many times and he heard me. I am now debt free and have an actual credit score with numbers.

I'm passionate about this topic because he can do it. Let go and trust in the Lord today. He will give you back anything that has been taken. He will bless your home and give you more than you can ask for or imagine.

Look for good in the darkness. The Lord can create a space of peace and beauty within the layers of confusion.

And this same God who takes care of me will supply all your needs from his glorious riches, which have been given to us in Christ Jesus.

PHILIPPIANS 4:19 NLT

God, please pour out your wisdom and direction as I trust you with my finances. Bring me provision so that I can extend generosity. I surrender my fears and place my faith in your ability to take care of me.

How can you trust God with your finances?

Journal

5

Beautiful Baggage

always hated the term *baggage*. I had heard it used a couple of times when I was in the dating world, and it always left a little dark cloud over me, like Pigpen from the Peanuts gang.

"I can see being married once, but twice? How did you manage to do that? That's a lot of baggage." That's just a taste of what I heard from the mouths of people who may have not dated me if I wasn't a singer doing background vocals with Carrie Underwood or performing on *The Tonight Show*. I'd come across some interesting people and would take in their negative words and wear them. I'll tell you what, when you keep hearing words that are degrading, you start to feel like a heavy Samsonite hard case that's been thrown around on a few too many turbulent flights. I started to believe that my story was way too complex and tricky to be something anyone would accept or not judge me for.

Had they known me, they'd know my whole story and that I was a victim of unfortunate circumstances, I would tell myself. *If I could just explain to them what happened and that I'm really a good person, maybe they wouldn't judge me.* The truth is, if you put on a white glove, you'll find a little dirt in any corner. But no matter how complicated and heavy you think your baggage is, it is never too heavy for God to carry. It doesn't matter what's inside that makes it difficult to hold; he just wants you to release the burden and trust him to do the heavy lifting.

Don't think of your life as a worn-out Samsonite, and don't let gripping lies form how you view your situation. Besides, there is nothing more beautiful than a parent who loves their children. Even if you've lived a "perfect life," someone somewhere will find some way you went wrong. None of us are free from others' opinions, and we need to listen to the voice that matters.

God tells us we are fearfully and wonderfully made, we're made in the image of Christ, we are sons and daughters of the King, and we are blessed and highly favored. Listen to the voice of the Father who holds no records of your wrongs and only sees your endless potential and beauty.

Beauty Mark

Change out the lens through which you view your life. Discover the undeniable beauty of who you are, and release the negative words or images you may have in your mind. You are more than enough.

> *For you created my inmost being; you knit me together in my mother's womb. I praise you because I am fearfully and wonderfully made; your works are wonderful, I know that full well. My frame was not hidden from you when I was made in the secret place, when I was woven together in the depths of the earth.*
>
> PSALM 139:13–15

God, help me see myself how you see me. As I surrender my negative thoughts, let positive words drown out the lies that have been spoken to me. Change my perspective so I'm able to see the beauty that is my life.

Be your own best friend. How would you talk to yourself if you were on the other side?

6

Unlearning

We are taught so many things throughout our lives, from the appropriate way to speak to others in public to who God is and how he sees us. The messages I received throughout my childhood affected my confidence and self-esteem after I had children. I was told about sin and shame, what not to do, how others are wrong, how missing a Sunday at church meant I didn't care as I should, and so on and so forth. As a child, I was even told to never wear my hair with a part down the middle because it made my face look too long. I actually didn't wear a middle part till my late twenties because of those words.

It's so easy for us to create standards that we hold on to for years, until we realize that we're holding on to false truths. I somehow felt that after my failed marriages and years of turmoil, God would no longer take pride in me like he did when I had my purity ring. I had been a part of such an extreme culture of judgment that I measured who I was and what I had done up against an impossible expectation of who I was supposed to be. I didn't even realize I was doing this because I never second-guessed my staple beliefs as being wrong. It's like these thoughts and ideas were carved in stone in my brain.

It's not easy to unlearn things. It's not easy to rewire. However, in time, this absolutely can be done. It took time, therapy, creating new habits, and asking God to show me who he was through all the noise. (And yes, I'm a huge advocate of counsel. I was raised to believe this was weakness, but it's quite the opposite.) I slowly learned that God was way different from some of his representatives. I had based my view of who he was on a family member treating me negatively or what I formed in my head after hearing an inaccurate sermon.

As soon as I read more about his grace and compassion, I began to view my situation through his eyes, and I slowly found that the shame started to fall off me. When I talked to people about my past, I could speak up with confidence and not give disclaimers because I knew I had nothing to fear since I knew I was loved and valued. Whatever you hold on to that keeps you from walking in confidence or valuing yourself, I encourage you to let it go and ask God to help you unlearn it.

Trust that God loves you so much. He adores you and sees the beauty within you and not your past choices.

Yet the LORD longs to be gracious to you; therefore he will rise up to show you compassion. For the LORD is a God of justice. Blessed are all who wait for him!

ISAIAH 30:18

Lord, help me know which thoughts and opinions are from your heart. Give me guidance through friendships, wise leaders, and your Word to help me see myself with the same eyes of compassion you have.

What is something you're unlearning?

Journal

7

Do You See What I See?

One of my favorite quotes by Maya Angelou is, "If you had known better, you would have done better." That has resonated with my heart on many occasions. As parents we can always look back and find ways we could've done things differently.

I was eighteen when I had my first baby, and boy was I not ready. Nor did I have any idea what being responsible for another human was like. I wanted to sleep till noon and hang with my friends. I had no family living with me in Nashville, so catching a break was nearly impossible.

Sometimes when I look back at the life my kids had, I see the places I wish I could change. Had I made more money, I could've given them more things. Or I could've afforded to stay in one place and not move constantly. I could've not gone through a messy divorce so they could've been spared the pain of a broken family. So many possibilities and what-ifs that I can never change. I think of moments when I could've done better, yet my children somehow see things way differently. My daughter is going to be eighteen this year, and she looks back fondly on memories of us "getting by."

As a born and raised Californian, Disneyland was a big deal for me. I couldn't afford to take my kids often, but we would go watch the fireworks at night—from outside of the park. One night in particular, we parked at a gas station, sat on the hood with blankets, and blasted some tunes. It ended up being a dance party and a night my daughter has never forgotten. She had no clue or care that we couldn't get into the park.

On another occasion, we were moving and only one person showed up to help me with a whole apartment of furniture and boxes. That one person had to leave early, and we were left with the rest of the U-Haul to unpack—just me and my nine-year-old. To top it off, halfway through the move it started to rain. Well, we ended up laughing hysterically and started yet another dance party through the puddles and downpour.

My daughter constantly tells me how she loved so many of the moments of what was not the easiest childhood. What I realize now is that our kids just want us: our love, our positivity, our humor, and our time. The real hang-out one-on-one meaningful loving time. You can always look back and see what you wish you could change or how you could've done better, but I promise you that simply doing the best *you* can is always enough. Your children will surprise you with all the things that brought them joy when you were seeing the heartache.

Beauty Mark

Do your best and make the most of every single moment. Your children will remember your efforts, and you'll have lasting, beautiful memories you'll cherish forever.

> *He hath made every thing beautiful in his time: also he hath set the world in their heart, so that no man can find out the work that God maketh from the beginning to the end.*
>
> ECCLESIASTES 3:11 KJV

Lord, help me live in the moment with my children. Give me clear vision to see all the ways you're making beautiful moments even through the difficulties. Give me grace for myself as I grow as a parent.

What is a fun, lighthearted activity you can do with your family?

8

Hello, Young Me

had a huge epiphany one day as I was discussing some of my fears with my therapist. I always considered myself to be a strong person. (I mean, I had the Japanese Kanji symbol for *brave* tattooed on my back over a decade ago, so that means I'm pretty brave, right?) But at times, I fall victim to my fears.

I can start with one simple topic in my mind and somehow end up sweeping ashes from a burning house. Then I jump out of it and realize I'm okay. Like, how do I even end up there? As I've gone through the stages of my life, I've recognized that on many occasions it was very difficult for me to resist fear. I was afraid I would die young like my brother did, I was afraid I would walk through a horrible situation with one of my children, I was afraid of failure, I was afraid of vulnerability, and, ultimately, I was afraid of being hurt.

My therapist asked me what I would tell the me from

ten years ago, the girl who was so afraid to live her fullest because she was a prisoner to the what-ifs. I proceeded to talk to my younger self and expressed compassion for the girl who was over-protective of herself. I told her that she would make it through and advised her to live life without fear because she certainly cannot control what happens.

My therapist then jumped to the older me ten years from now. She said, "What do you think she would tell you in this very moment? Probably those very same things you just told the younger you. To let go, stop worrying, trust that there's a plan for your life; you will make it through." This was a big moment for me. I surely don't want to walk through the next ten years worrying about things that may never happen and are clearly out of my control.

Being a single parent can sometimes wreak havoc on your brain waves. Being a mother in itself can cause anxieties to surface that you'd never imagine you'd have. My youngest is two, and I still find myself creeping into her room at night, placing my hand on her back, and making sure she's okay. There's simply too much that's out of our hands, and we can't predict or control every situation. The one thing we have control of is our perspective. You can choose to look at your life with eyes of fear, or you can choose to put your trust in God and save yourself the heartache of living through hypothetical scenarios that most likely will never happen.

Wherever you're at in this very moment, I encourage you to release your fears and allow God to truly be in control. It's never easy to let go when we want to brace for impact. The Lord wants us to be free from worry and fear. The Bible is so clear about casting our cares on him and how worry will not add a single hour to our life. It only hurts our mind, harms our heart, and takes a toll on our physical health.

Beauty
Mark

Don't be upset about time wasted with worry. Know that in this very moment, you can change the course of your future by simply putting your trust in God and allowing him to take over.

> *Then Jesus said to His disciples, "Therefore I tell you, do not worry about your life, what you will eat, or about your body, what you will wear. For life is more than food, and the body more than clothes. Consider the ravens: They do not sow or reap; they have no storehouse or barn, yet God feeds them. How much more valuable are you than the birds! Who of you by worrying can add a single hour to his lifespan?"*
>
> LUKE 12:22–25 BSB

God, I release to you my worries and fears. Help me trust that you have things figured out. I pray to move forward with a new beginning. Let this be the day where everything changes.

What encouragement would you give
to a younger you, and what do you think
the older you would say to you today?

Journal

9

I See Your True Colors

s much as I think I'm above the petty things, I can occasionally be dragged into caring about stuff that doesn't matter. It's easy to say that I'm strong in who I am and no amount of slander can affect me. But it does.

When I was going through a difficult divorce, I was shaken to the core by some of the cruel accusations made in court. There were blown-up Myspace pictures of me with rocker hair (from a cover band show) and duck lips while I made a peace sign. It wasn't my best shot, but it certainly wasn't the portrait of a bad mother, as the lawyer had stated. The lies under oath also shook me to the core. I had told myself before this court day that I would not fabricate anything in the slightest. I wouldn't stoop to lower levels, and I would hope for truth to prevail.

Truth, however, did not prevail that September day. In fact, it ended up being one of the most gut-wrenching, air-sucked-out-of-my-lungs days in my whole life. You see, I didn't have the money to build the kind of case I could have. My ex-husband's mother retained the best child custody lawyer in Nashville, and they sure backed me into a corner. By the end of the case, I think anyone would have been convinced that a musician shouldn't procreate.

It was devastating. I can only look back and see how God delivered me from this very dark moment. I flew to Florida constantly to see my son, as my ex had primary residential custody. I sent monthly child support checks and nearly lived on a street corner trying to juggle the insanity.

Sometimes our vindication doesn't come when we want it to. People may believe negative things about you and try to tarnish your character. I still remember a Facebook comment one of my ex's cousins made under our picture: "What will her wedding dress color be next time? Brown?" It stayed with me, as did the lies that were spoken in court.

God never ever let me fall. Through the moments of distance between my son and the pain that cut my heart like a knife, I know beyond the shadow of a doubt that his love was with me and I was never alone. I also had a strong belief that all things in time would be revealed. As I stayed the course, I would see how every single lie and accusation, every assumption others had, and every horrible character assassination was dissolved. I didn't receive a miracle overnight, but God was faithful to bring justice to my situation in the most beautiful way.

My son is now with me! I missed out on some things, but this time I now have with him is beyond special. It's like I'm making up for the lost time and then some. There was no lie that wasn't overthrown. No evil that wasn't dealt with.

Trust today that any evil that has tried to take you down will be overthrown by the truth of who you are in Christ. Know that in time God can redeem your life from the lies and set you up for a win that's bigger than you imagined. Know that the thoughts he has for you are good thoughts. Rest in the truth—the truth of who you know you are, and the truth of who God knows you to be.

Beauty Mark

Block out the words and lies that are trying to shake you. Imagine the Lord's love like a sealant around you so nothing can absorb into your spirit. God will not fail you; he will make a way through the darkness to lift you up.

> *"For the LORD will vindicate His people, and will have compassion on His servants, when He sees that their strength is gone, and there is none remaining, bond or free."*
>
> DEUTERONOMY 32:36 NASB

Lord, give me the strength to hold on to your promises. Help me cling to the truth when lies want to bring me down. I know you're faithful to resolve all conflict and dissolve any injustice against me.

Write down some truths about you that counter any lies that have been spoken about your life.

10

Big Little Things

hen I used to travel more extensively, I would share a little story before singing one of my songs. When my oldest daughter was transitioning from a bassinet to a crib, I decided to do a little day of shopping. This involved a few different stores and stops. Throughout the day, the most random things continued to happen.

At my first stop, I was walking back to the car and realized there were a couple of DVDs underneath the cart that I hadn't paid for. After throwing my items into the trunk of the car, I took the DVDs and went back into the store to let them know I needed to pay for them. The lady was quite surprised by this and thanked me for my honesty.

The next stop was Target. I threw together the items of the new baby room, and as I left the store, there was yet again something that they did not charge me for. Now this item wasn't too expensive, so I questioned even bringing it back in. My conscience got the best of me, and I knew I just wouldn't feel good about leaving without paying. I clearly remember they were striped toe socks. I ran these back into the store and shared with the lady that the socks somehow ended up in my cart without being paid for. She was pleasantly surprised, thanked me for my honesty, and off I went for my last purchase of the day.

It was now time to purchase the new crib my growing girl needed. I was on a tight budget and wasn't happy that I had to drop a couple hundred on this item, but it was necessary. The store was getting ready to close, and I ran to get into the line. So much was happening, and I handed over my card and signed without even thinking. As I walked out, I knew something wasn't right. I looked at the receipt and saw that they only charged me ten dollars for the crib.

So, after doing the right thing all day, I decided to run for it. Just kidding. I thought about it, I'll be honest, but I went back into the store and talked to the lady at guest services. I explained how they *way* undercharged me and that I needed to pay the difference. She got on the phone with her manager, and when she got off, she said that the manager wanted me to have the crib at the price they charged me for it and that they thanked me for my honesty.

Even when we feel like certain choices don't matter, they really do. If you are faithful in the little things, God will bless you and trust you with so much. God always had a way of giving me a wink and a nod. From his faithfulness to uphold me, to his generosity to always provide what we needed, he has never failed me. Always honor the Lord with the little things, and I promise you will see his goodness in all the areas of your life.

Honesty and truth stir up beauty from within us that can be seen by others. Give the Lord your best by being faithful in all things, as he will remain faithful to us.

> *Look at the birds of the air: They do not sow or reap or gather into barns—and yet your Heavenly Father feeds them. Are you not much more valuable than they?*
>
> MATTHEW 6:26 BSB

God, help me trust you in every detail of my life. Thank you for your generosity and faithfulness to me.

What are some ways God has
shown kindness to you?

Journal

11

What Do I Have?

There's always someone who has more than we do. Someone who is experiencing more cool events or eating fancier meals. With the power of social media, we can pretty much see every detail of someone's life—well, every detail they want us to see. We can compare almost anything, from vacations to shoes.

Sometimes we find ourselves thinking about all the things we don't have. I work in the music industry, and it can be a competitive place that breeds insecurities and doubts. I constantly have to remind myself to stay in my own lane because I'm going where the Lord wants me to go. It's a journey no one else can take.

I have to remind myself to focus on gratitude. I guarantee you there is always something you can find in your life to be thankful for. It could be a parent who is helpful, a friend who you can trust, a healthy child, or breath in your lungs.

Just as we can see an Instagram of the best of someone's life, if there were an Instagram where we could see the worst of someone's life, I'm sure we'd realize that there is someone fighting through the same circumstance as us or something even more difficult.

By showing thankfulness to God for everything we *do* have, we are worshiping him. Gratitude is like injecting peace into your soul while comparison is like poison. The toxicity of envy will forever leave you empty. It's impossible to function in this mind-set without constantly activating feelings of inadequacy. If you place your happiness in accumulating things, you'll never experience fullness of joy. There's always more you could have and always someone who will have it.

I've been on opposite sides of the fence on several occasions. I actually look back fondly on the times when I was without and life was uncertain. I found simplicity and fun in those uncertain moments.

Whether it's leaving your phone on the counter for the day or enjoying a fun Friday night at home because you can't find a sitter, sometimes by getting rid of some clutter we're able to concentrate on little everyday moments that we may not have recognized otherwise. If you create space in your life to be present, you'll soon begin to recognize, through the beauty in the little things, all the ways God is around you.

There are so many areas of our lives where we can find beauty. Open your eyes to the simple things that make you smile.

Do not be conformed to this world, but be transformed by the renewal of your mind, that by testing you may discern what is the will of God, what is good and acceptable and perfect.

ROMANS 12:2 ESV

Lord, help me see the goodness in every area of my life. I thank you for everything I have and for the simple joys that surround me. Fill my heart and mind with your love so that I may rest in your perfect peace.

Write down some simple things you are grateful for and acknowledge God's goodness in your life.

12

What If ...
Everything Works Out?

hat if everything you're holding on to and all your fears never come to life? What if, ten years from now, you're actually getting along with your ex and your kids are happy and thriving? What if everything you're worrying about today is a total and complete waste of the energy you could share with you children?

I'll probably circle this topic a few times through this devotional because I feel like, for moms, worry and fear will always try to creep in somewhere. We have to be strong against this. What-if scenarios are not only draining but they're also time consuming and life sucking. We can lay our head on the pillow after a long, tiring day, and before we know it, we're not resting at all.

Rewiring and reprogramming the brain is not an overnight

process. We have to be aware when those thoughts creep in so we can slowly start to switch the program that's been playing in our thoughts. When you find yourself dwelling on the thought of your child choking on a piece of food that the babysitter didn't cut small enough or your teenager doing something behind your back, or when you worry about whether your kids are safe at school or with a friend, you're actually putting stress on your body. Stress that is completely unnecessary when this hypothetical situation hasn't even happened. You're stimulating stress responses that harm you, and nothing bad has even happened.

You don't need to walk through trauma when you're not in danger. (I sometimes need to repeat this to myself.) Take the next *what-if* thought that tries to force its way into your brain and replace it with *what is*. My child is safe at school right now, my child is in the care of a responsible person, I am not alone, I am healthy and alive, things are not hopeless. As you start being present in the real moment, you can dwell on the truth of where your life is and what things are worth your energy.

What if everything comes together for the good? What if God is ordering all your steps and directing your path? What if you'll come through your situation stronger and better? Focus on the *what is* and exchange all the what-ifs with something positive. Even if you're tempted to allow your mind to fear something you think could really happen, remind yourself of the truth and allow that to lead your thoughts.

Focus on the simple joys in your life. Don't allow negative thoughts to creep in and steal your peace.

Watch over your heart with all diligence, for from it flow the springs of life.

PROVERBS 4:23 NASB

Lord, I ask you to be near me as I watch over my heart. Help me be present with my family and love in the moment. Help me think thoughts of positivity and hope.

Write down what is going on in your life that is joyful and hopeful.

Journal

13

Reach Out

ost of my time as a single mom was spent thousands of miles away from friends and family. I was a loner and kind of started to take that on as my thing. Just the loner single mom who can do it all on her own. I was too prideful to reach out because, in my young eyes, I believed that meant I couldn't handle life—that I had gotten myself into the situation and it was my job to have it all covered. At times I believed that by asking for help, I was a failure and I deserved to experience any inconvenience and hardship that came with the territory. To put it simply, I was punishing myself.

Asking for help seemed more painful than a hammer to the finger. I would've chosen to experience physical pain rather than possibly be told no after being vulnerable enough to ask for something. With the painful upbringing I experienced, I almost always braced for impact when it came to friends and relationships. I assumed the worst and felt like it would only be a matter of time before someone let me down or broke my heart.

Along my journey, I met a couple of women who pursued me. They just wouldn't let me go. One in particular was an angel to me and my children, and now she's in heaven. She said, "People love you. They want to help you. Let us help pick up the slack." And boy did she! She moved to Nashville and became a constant source of help for the couple of years she lived near me before she passed. She was a grandma to my children, and my daughter still talks fondly about this woman who impacted her young life. Michelle had no genetic ties to my kids, but her love and the mark she left on their hearts was bigger than any left by a distant family member.

There are people who are ready to be in your life. You may think you're taking from them, but for people who may not have family of their own, you could be equally giving to them. Whether that person is a mentor to help show you the ropes of parenting, a new friend who can help with some school drop-offs, another single mom to vent to about the strains of parenting solo, or just a fun person to connect and escape with for a bit, there are people out there who can fill some of the relational voids in your life.

I've often seen people post on Facebook, being vulnerable about needing friendships and support, and you'd be surprised by the overwhelming amount of people who can serve *your* need. People and resources are available for whatever need you may be experiencing, such as support groups, online forums, church small groups, and ways you can expand your community. Relationships can be key in life, joy, business, and growth in your family.

Allow vulnerability and authenticity to take the lead when building your community. By opening up to others, you'll see the beauty that is all around you. There are wonderful people who are looking for someone like you in their life.

> *Finally, all of you, be like-minded, be sympathetic, love one another, be compassionate and humble.*
>
> I PETER 3:8

God, help me open my heart to new friendships. When I experience needs in my life, please align me with the right people who can help me carry my burden.

What are some ways you can open your circle and expand your friendships? Is there a need you have right now that you can reach out and talk to someone about?

14

What You See
Is What You Get

I used to find myself sugarcoating parts of my story depending on who I was talking to, especially when I was dating. My daughter would ask me, "Did you drop the mom bomb yet?" The *mom bomb*? That sounds so negative. But based on some of the judgments she and I encountered in the process, it wasn't too farfetched. Having to tell someone I had been married twice and had two kids was not an easy thing to do. I would always hope they would Google me first, because my past was detailed in several places, including Wikipedia. I used to hate that anyone can know all about my life, but I actually found some positivity in it. If someone ended up canceling without a raincheck, I knew I had been Googled.

Telling your story is so personal. You may have experienced judgment yourself, or you could be a fortunate soul who has had endless support (which is something to be so thankful for). I was apprehensive and terrified of who I was. Because I was so hard on myself, how could I ever imagine someone seeing me with eyes of grace and understanding?

Here I am. All of me. All my flaws. All my failures. I can't go back and change a single thing, and I certainly wouldn't change the fact that I have amazing babies that bring me endless joy. It took me a while to reach this confidence and understanding with myself, but oh the freedom that came when I did.

In any type of relationship, whether it's friendship, work related, or romantic, we can challenge ourselves to be authentically who we are. In a world of airbrush and autotune, people are starving for what is real. I even have friends who've had such smooth sailing in their lives that they're afraid to share with people that they haven't had too many bumps in their road. There is always a flip side to everything. Now I can't relate to the smooth sailing, but I appreciate the realness of saying, "What do I possibly have that someone else can connect with?" Well, chances are if you've lived it, someone else has too.

Sometimes when I'm meeting people for the first time, I can draw a quick conclusion in my head. *Oh, wow, she looks like she has it all together. She probably won't connect with me.*

I bet she met her husband in high school and everything has been perfect. She definitely won't like me. Most of the time I end up being completely wrong. A couple of hours into a get-together, one person shares something vulnerable, and before I know it, I've said, "Me too," so many times. I've had to learn to give people more grace and space to be authentic with me as well. This occurs way more often when I am being 100 percent me without sugarcoating a thing. Real attracts real!

I challenge you. No matter what your story is, don't be afraid to share it. You'll find a personal freedom in being authentic, but you'll also offer a space of freedom to others. Your story could help create an atmosphere of change and connection to so many around you.

By being open and authentic about your past, you're opening yourself to encouragement from others and a chance to experience freedom from judging yourself. Lasting connections can be made through vulnerability and showing love to others.

> *Now the Lord is the Spirit, and where the Spirit of the Lord is, there is freedom.*
>
> 2 CORINTHIANS 3:17

Lord, help me love myself and others with the unconditional love that you give. Thank you for your never-ending well of grace. Help me have confidence in who I am and help me see my past as a gift to others.

What are some pieces of your past
that you're ready to let go of?

Journal

15

Realistic Hope

fter having my third child, I started to deal with a little life pain called chronic migraines. When they start to set in, I become frustrated because whatever I have planned for the rest of the day is most likely now questionable.

Sometimes I become anxious and question what my life is about simply based on one bad day. This bad day can even have the power to make me become negative and forget that the difficult time will eventually pass. It may take a couple of days to get over the hump, but the headache does eventually go away and I'm back to life as usual. The clouds disappear and hope feels a little more realistic.

Hope doesn't always look and feel realistic, but it's a huge reality. When I was a new parent, some days were entirely overwhelming, and it seemed like my baby would never sleep through a night. For a few months, I thought my child would never stop throwing a tantrum and trying to give a

TKO with her flailing hands. I would count down the hours to her bedtime because I knew I would finally get a reprieve. And eventually, I always did find some solitude.

Whatever stage your life or children are in, you can't lose sight of hope. No matter how bad things may seem today, no matter how exhausted you are, there will be spaces of peace for you. Sometimes they come to you, and sometimes you have to take initiative to find them.

I have many friends who are either dealing with uncertainties in their child's learning development or navigating the road of autism. The amount of grace and patience they have astounds me, and it's a beautiful thing to see all the love overflowing from these families. My dear friend explains how some days are so trying that she feels patience wearing thin and life swallowing her whole, and the next day her creative, adorable son who has autism rests his hand on her cheek and tells her she's a beautiful mommy. It's in those moments that she's renewed. She finds beauty in the chaos of her life with the sweet simplicity of her son's unconditional love.

Don't allow negative thoughts to swallow you whole today. Trust that these will pass and you will find a moment of peace. Maybe those moments will stretch out longer and longer till you find that you've successfully walked through a trial and come out of it even stronger.

Look for the beauty in the chaos. Trust that life will bring to you moments of rest and rejuvenation so you can continue to be the incredible woman you are.

> *Come unto me, all ye that labour and are heavy laden, and I will give you rest.*
>
> MATTHEW 11:28 KJV

God, I ask you for peace and rest in my home. Help me have hope in all circumstances and fully trust that you will walk me through the moments that leave me exhausted.

How can you carve out some time
to have moments of rest?

16

Be Who You Wanted

t the beginning of my mothering journey, I didn't have much of a clue about what I was doing. I had siblings who were way younger than me and I'd looked after them quite a bit, but as far as being what my kids needed emotionally, I didn't have it all figured out. I would say that I couldn't do certain things because I hadn't been taught to be that way or I hadn't received that sort of thing as a child. I was simply making excuses because I was uncomfortable (but yes, there were things I didn't receive from my parents as a child).

I could have definitely stayed the course of excuses. It would've been the easy road, but it would've led to harder situations, for myself and my kids. I had to do the old oxygen-mask-on-myself-first and then start to be to my kids what I didn't know how to be. I later realized that the things that made me feel so terribly awkward were the things I probably really needed growing up.

For me it was physical affection. My mom tended to hug me without a grip. An awkward pat-on-the-back kind of hug. I would do this to my kids. A weird pat on the head and a cryptic embrace you might not even feel. I started to see the patterns and recognize my awkwardness. Soon I discovered it was time for me to extend love to them in a way that made me uncomfortable. I now do a ninja-grip bear hug that they can't escape. It didn't change overnight, but I eventually started recognizing my patterns and seeing the places in me that I needed to change. For me and my kids.

Bear hugs may not be an issue for you, but maybe you were never asked for your opinion as a child. Did you feel invisible? Maybe you were raised by someone who yelled a lot, and now you struggle with admitting you're wrong. Pride and fear of failure can also make parenting an uphill climb. Whatever it is that keeps you from experiencing freedom in your parenting, I challenge you to look within. There are so many patterns and habits that are a part of our instinctual parenting and we don't even realize it. I didn't realize it till my little girl told me to hug her tighter in her sweet little toddler voice.

I continually have to remind myself to be to my children the parent I wanted as a child. Did I want a long hug? Did I want to be asked my opinion? Did I want an apology when something went wrong? Our kids are little humans who are thinking, feeling, and evolving every day. You are setting the example of how they will someday treat your grandbabies. This is why we need to handle with such care.

Change can happen in any moment. You can create something beautiful in your children's lives that will make a lasting impact even if you've already made mistakes.

Put on then, as God's chosen ones, holy and beloved, compassionate hearts, kindness, humility, meekness, and patience.
COLOSSIANS 3:12 ESV

God, I ask that you continually teach me how to be the best parent I can be. Help me show love and understanding to my precious kids. Let me make a difference that changes generations.

What did you want as a child from your parents, and how can you do that now?

Journal

17

All by Myself ...
Don't Wanna Be

*L*oneliness can be a real struggle. When your child does something extraordinarily cute and you want to tell someone about it immediately, when the kids are asleep and the house is super quiet, and when the weight of your responsibilities are overwhelming and you could use a teammate to help with the heavy lifting—these are just some of the many times we're reminded that we're flying solo.

I went through a time of isolating myself because I didn't know how to interact in groups without having someone with me. I remember spending a New Year's Eve in bed listening to "Moon River" on repeat and planning on bringing in the new year asleep. (I actually fell asleep before midnight last year too, lol!) My kids were away for the night, and I felt so terribly alone.

I had been invited to a gathering at a friend's house but decided not to go, knowing people would be kissing at midnight and I would be alone in a corner feeling completely awkward. Well, 11:40 came, and something in me decided to jump out of bed and drive down the street to the party before midnight hit. That ended up being a great decision. Yes, I did semi-stare at the ceiling at the stroke of midnight, but when everyone was done with their smooch session, I was back in the celebration surrounded by some really cool people.

There may be times when you feel like you can conquer the world, and other times when the fact that you're doing all of this alone is highlighted by some couples' get-together or some other little reminder that a partner is not present. You may have been doing this alone from the very beginning of your parenting journey, and you'd love to know what a partnership and teammate in parenting feels like. No matter where you are, you don't have to let parenting alone bring you down.

To be honest, there are so many moments I now look back on so fondly. A few things were actually easier for me. You will experience times of loneliness in life, but people experience that even when they have a partner. We have to be brave when those emotions arise and look for spaces of beauty within our lives. Some mothers decide to do it alone the whole way through. They do the very best they can, and their children are remarkably well-adjusted and adore their mom.

Whether you long for a partner or a family, long for a friend, or feel a bit disconnected, you can rest in the fact that God knows every detail of your story and he is weaving it into a beautiful tapestry. You may go through various seasons of change and transition, but he is there with you on the journey. The pieces you desire to have in your life are not too far from reach. There is joy to be found all around you. Take in every moment because it truly does fly by.

These are the moments to take in and savor. You will one day look back at this time in your life with gratitude and fondness. Don't miss out on the beauty of your life while looking for what's next.

> A *cheerful heart is good medicine, but a crushed spirit dries up the bones.*
>
> PROVERBS 17:22

God, help me live in these moments with joy and expecta-tion. Help me find completion in you when it feels like there are voids in my life.

What are some voids in your life
that you'd like God to fill?

18

The Thing

hroughout many moments in my life, I was always waiting for *the thing*. *The thing* could've been achieving musical success, moving into my own house, selling a song to someone amazing, finding the man of my dreams, or taking the next big life step that would bring me to financial freedom and outward validation of my career path. I often overlooked the exact place where I stood: who was around me, what was around me, what I was learning, and how I was growing. I could only focus on where I wanted to be. In my brain I created this category of what it would be like when I was finally there.

So where's *there*? I'm still figuring that out.

I look back and, like when Glinda told Dorothy (in *The Wizard of Oz*) that she had the power in her shoes all along, I realize I had the power in my shoes too. I was constantly trying to figure out ways to get to the destination and missed out on the incredible journey—the process of refining, the process of learning, the beauty of the stages in my children's lives, the magical music moments, and the places I was able to see. While waiting for the dream to happen, I was actually living the dream.

As I look back on those times when I was complacent and waiting for a breakthrough, I realize that some of those moments were, in fact, the best of my life so far. I could name countless ways that God was so evident in my life.

God knows the deepest desires of our heart. He knew my biggest dream was to help people. Had I not walked through the difficulties of my past, I probably would not have learned all the things God wanted to teach me so I could have wisdom in that area. My healing didn't happen overnight; it took time and oh so much patience. But that's the difference between a miracle and a healing. Some miracles are instantaneous, but when God heals your spirit, it's usually a process. God healed my heart and mind of so many wounds. But it was the journey that was the important part of my path. Now it's the journey that brings me so much joy and gratitude. The uncertainty and pain were actually connecting me to God's heart.

What you're doing in this moment is *the thing*. This is where you should be, and this is where you should focus. Don't let life breeze by while you're hoping and waiting for what's next. Focus on your family, focus on your heart, and focus on the process of healing. Allow God to fill every fiber of your being with his love, and trust that he is refining you in a way that will bring you to the desires of your heart. I promise that whatever he has to teach you is far more valuable than jumping right into your perfect dream. Let his love and teaching be your place of rest.

Allow yourself to take in this very moment. Allow the present to be your focus. There is beauty all around you. Don't worry about tomorrow or next year; relax, breathe in, and look at your life through eyes of gratitude.

Delight thyself also in the LORD: and he shall give thee the desires of thine heart. Commit thy way unto the LORD; trust also in him; and he shall bring it to pass.

PSALM 37:4–5 KJV

God, I trust that I am exactly where I'm supposed to be. Heal my heart of any wounds that haven't closed, and let this process bring me to a better understanding of who you are and who I am.

What is something that you want to happen
that you've been praying for?
How can you find God in the waiting?

Journal

19

Change Will Do Ya Good

*T*oday is an opportunity—a chance to see something new, a time to learn, a day to set goals, a moment to reflect, a choice to embrace gratitude, and a day to open your heart and mind to see all things beautiful.

So many of my big life changes happened in a single moment. Now the process to the goal took time, but my choices happened in an instant. In a moment I was able to decide that I was ready to be disciplined in my diet. I laid my head down on my pillow and said, "Tomorrow will be different. I will choose to put only good things in my mouth, and I will make a change." I didn't lose that forty pounds right away, but on that night, I made a choice that truly changed the path of my health and well-being. Forever. One day I decided to stop dating self-centered jerks. Another day I decided to put my fear on the back burner and fully trust God (I'm still on that journey). Another day I decided to inch by inch get out of debt and start the process to financial freedom; a few years after that, I was no longer in the red.

You may be discouraged and think things can't change overnight, but they can. You can make a firm decision in this very moment that will be a defining change for the rest of your life. You can set a goal and stick to it. Even if you have a bad day and get off course, you can get right back on the path to achieving your goals. Don't let a bad meal choice steer you away from living your best. Don't let a moment of frustration make you think you're doing a bad job with parenting. You can react in a way that doesn't make you happy and then choose to make a different decision the next time.

An all-or-nothing mentality really hurt me in my process of finding myself. I had no room for error, so I figured nobody had grace for me. How could I believe people would accept me, flaws and all, if I didn't accept myself? This was a defining change that helped me move forward in my life and find freedom. We can't move toward change if we beat ourselves up along the way. We must accept that to change our lives and redefine how we see ourselves, we have to have room for error.

You possess the tools needed to move forward. God has more than enough love and strength to fill your heart for the journey. Whatever may be keeping you from fully believing you can live your life with fullness and purpose is simply a lie that you have the power to toss aside.

Beauty Mark

You have everything you need within you to redirect your path to reaching your goals and dreams. Find the beauty in your errors and keep on moving forward.

See, I am doing a new thing! Now it springs up; do you not perceive it? I am making a way in the wilderness and streams in the wasteland.

ISAIAH 43:19

God, help me love myself the way you love me. Thank you for your unending grace and forgiveness. Let this be a day of defining change as I fully trust in you.

What is something you can start in this very moment that can change your life?

20

Dream *Big* and
Bring a Juice Box

Some people find it so very easy to project their opinions about what parenting should look like. Moms should stay at home, kids need to be in pajamas by six p.m., homeschooling is bad, public schools are bad, private schools are bad. I've heard something negative about everything—even things you'd think someone couldn't find something negative about. There's always someone with an opposing opinion, and you must be wise in who you allow to speak into your life and dreams. I've seen good friends convince wives to stay in their marriage, and I've seen good friends convince them to leave. There is power in opinions if you allow them to dictate how you live.

When it comes to dreams, my opinions once had the power to control my decisions. While in court, I was once told that music was a selfish ambition that was fueled by my need for attention—certainly not an example a young child should follow. Had I listened to those voices, I wouldn't have sung one hundred and fifty off-camera songs for the show *Glee*, done the fun background vocal sessions for awesome artists, shared the stage with Prince, or been a semi-finalist on *America's Got Talent*. These were moments that surprised me in a huge pinch-myself kind of way. Darkness wanted to keep me bound to others' opinions and break my dreams; it wanted to convince me I was a too-old, too-washed-up, too-much-baggage-carrying girl who should go home and bake a cake. Now I can bake an awesome cake, but I'll do it while I'm moving forward.

When I would go on dates, guys were often perplexed that I had kids and a full-time job. It was like this weird, otherworldly thing for some people. I've also experienced the stigmas related to music, dream chasing, and parenting. I just chose to never listen. It was never easy. But I've done a lot of traveling with my kids, and they've seen and experienced so many amazing things in their life through the excitement of what I get to do. It was never a traditional situation, but it was ours.

Don't be afraid. The only thing you should fear is going through life with regret for not embracing your dreams. The children of women I've met who never took time for their passions were far more upset for their mothers than the children of those who took time to pursue what they loved. Don't allow fear to shut the door on your ambitions. Being a mother is an awesome job that takes time, love, and guidance, but you can do this *and* be a dream chaser. I promise you can do it all. Nothing in your life has to come to a screeching halt. Assemble your team, get creative, reach out for help, and pack up the kids. Get going on your journey and don't look back.

Your dreams are waiting for you. Push fears aside and don't attach your mind-set to doubts that you can't accomplish what you set your heart to do.

> *So do not fear, for I am with you; do not be dismayed, for I am your God. I will strengthen you and help you; I will uphold you with my righteous right hand.*
>
> ISAIAH 41:10

God, help me navigate my steps, and set me free from fear. Bring people into my life who can aid me in pursuing my passion. Give me patience for the ride and energy to see it through.

What are some goals you have that you've been putting off? How can you fearlessly accomplish them?

Journal

21

The Freedom of Discipline

hen I was raising my older kids, I thought of discipline and structure as chains that could prohibit me from living to my fullest. I didn't set a bedtime, didn't meal plan, and pretty much didn't plan ahead on much of anything. But I learned that this made my life a chaotic mess. I'm not saying you can't successfully do what you need to do without a set bedtime. I'm suggesting, from personal experience, that setting some boundaries in my life set me free. It set my kids free too.

By setting a bedtime, I was able to work at night and my kids were much happier the next day. By planning ahead with meals, activities, and chores, I was able to better predict (in the best way a mom can) how my days would pan out. And I would follow through with every disciplinary threat. Always.

One time my daughter and I were at Chuck E. Cheese's

and she was acting up in front of her friends. I told her if she continued, I would pack everything up and we would leave. She didn't believe I would inconvenience myself to the point that I'd pack up fresh pizza *and* drive her friends home. Well, I did. We didn't even touch the pizza. We packed it up, I sent it with her friends with some consolation prizes and a raincheck, and we went home. I can tell you this: after that, any time I ever told her to stop acting up, she listened. Even to this day, my children know to ask once and that's all. If their friends try to convince them to beg me, my kids tell them, "No. Mom already gave an answer."

Sometimes discipline is an inconvenience for us too. Like when I take away my teenage daughter's cell phone and then I can't reach her after school if I'm running late or something. It's entirely worth it though. Knowing there are rules gives them a sense of security and assurance that I care, and it also gives some structure to our life.

This may be a boring chapter for you; I even wondered if I should include it in the book. But when I thought about the things that helped me the most in parenting, this was one of them. So here it is. And if you're a planner, then this chapter will be a can-I-get-an-amen for you. Take some time and evaluate the things that are overwhelming your life and heart. Recognize the areas that need some structure and how you can create it to bring yourself peace of mind. Whether it's scheduling a nap for your toddler while you read a book you've been wanting to read or putting dinner in the slow cooker in the morning so it's one less thing to fuss about after a long day, there are ways to simplify your life so you can walk in the fullness of what is out there for you. Yes, parenting takes a ton of your time, but there are ways to capture moments that are yours.

Years ago, my sister-in-law had to come over to help me after my child had been sleeping with me for fourteen months and had never slept through a night. I'm totally for co-sleeping, but in this case, I wasn't sleeping. On the first night in her crib, my poor child fell asleep standing up because she didn't know she was supposed to lie down. I was a wreck and she was in heaven. By night three, this little angel was sleeping from seven at night until seven in the morning! I didn't know what to do with myself. She was happier and I was too. I missed our time together, but I'll always cherish the closeness of that first year.

In whatever area you need structure, I encourage you to take some steps to create it. There is freedom on the other side that can lead you into working on your dreams, finding rest and recovery, having more patience with your children, or just getting to bed earlier.

You have the ability to bring a little peace in the midst of chaos. By taking some time to structure a program for your family, you can create space and freedom to fulfill your dreams and passions.

> *Do not be anxious about anything, but in every situation, by prayer and petition, with thanksgiving, present your requests to God. And the peace of God, which transcends all understanding, will guard your hearts and your minds in Christ Jesus.*
> PHILIPPIANS 4:6–7

Lord, I ask for your wisdom and guidance in raising my family. Help me decipher what is best for myself and my children. Give us new ideas to create freedom and balance in our life.

What are some things you can change
that would make your life easier?

22

Big Boo-Boos
and Brown Sugar

ids aren't the only ones who make mistakes. Some little, some big, some dumb, and some dumber. We are all human, so it's inevitable that we will not do things perfectly. That's a fact.

To make it through the boo-boos, you must have grace for yourself and embrace transparency. There were times when I had to sit my daughter down and ask for her understanding when I didn't quite get it right. Ten times out of ten, she was willing to give it, and she felt like her little heart mattered in our situation.

Parenting is not easy. We weren't given a manual, and we especially weren't given a manual on how to do it alone. You can't truly prepare for what bumps will be in the road, so sit back and take a deep breath, knowing you're doing the best you can.

I remember a time when I lost my cool in front of my daughter. I'd let her attitude overwhelm me when I was figuring out how to stay afloat, and I'd snap or say something I'd regret. There are so many ways we can believe that we fall short.

I'll also never forget the morning my toddler decided to take matters into her own hands. Still a teenager at the time, I was in a phase of wanting to sleep in. I loved my sleep, and it was so hard for me to wake up early. Like, nearly impossible at times. I would turn on TV cartoons in my bedroom, and she would lay next to me in bed and eat Cheerios while I slept.

Well, one morning I guess I was so exhausted from working that I didn't wake up at all. I didn't hear her until she walked into the room to wake me up. Holding a bowl of brown sugar and a spoon, she said, "Don't worry, Mom. I made breckfix." Oh boy, was that a wake-up call! I felt so bad. For days I kicked myself, feeling sad that my daughter felt that she needed to pick up some pieces to help me.

After that, I set my alarm and pushed myself to be more present. Even when my body wanted to shut down and I couldn't keep my eyes open. The me of today would now go back fifteen years and tell the young me that it's okay, that I was tired and had a lot on my plate with no help, and that I just needed to pick up and move forward. Unfortunately,

I went around feeling like a bad mom. I could only concentrate on where I was going wrong instead of on what I was doing right.

Your kids may not be eating brown sugar today, but maybe you feel like a rubber band that's stretching and getting so thin that you may snap. You may feel like you're on the edge of what you can handle and may be beating yourself up for not being Superwoman. Maybe you even blame yourself for circumstances in your life. Well, it's time to put shame, self-doubt, guilt, and regret in the back seat. In fact, just throw them out the window!

You are an overcomer. You are bettering yourself to be the best parent that you can be, you are pushing through a tough situation, and you are still standing. Be proud of the things you are doing and have grace in the areas you feel are lacking.

Love and transparency will go a long way with your children. Giving them your time and hearing them out will assure you that when they're older, they'll have respect for you and understanding of what you went through to raise them.

My brown sugar story is now a funny memory my daughter occasionally shares. As a seventeen-year-old young woman, she can't imagine raising a daughter now. She says, "I don't know how you did it. I need my life and my sleep." She gets it. I also see her and have grace for my teenage self. How *did* I do it? Ha! By the grace of God, you surely can.

Beauty
Mark

Be kind to yourself today. Have grace and kindness toward yourself, as you're doing your best to be a wonderful parent. Find the joy and beauty in the mistakes and use them as an opportunity to connect with your child.

> *Let us then approach God's throne of grace with confidence, so that we may receive mercy and find grace to help us in our time of need.*
>
> HEBREWS 4:16

God, thank you that your grace is never-ending. Help me connect with my children through communication, love, and understanding. Give me opportunities to teach them lessons and let them feel loved and heard.

Where do you feel you're lacking as a parent, and how can you show yourself grace?

Journal

23

Maddy

y daughter went through a season when she decided to call me Maddy. She was feeling a lack in her life and wanted to be able to have both a mom and a dad. She told people, "She's my Maddy. My Mommy Daddy." It was really sweet. It also added a little pressure. In my crazy mind at the time, I believed that I needed to better embody all of what she could want, in the most stereotypical ways possible.

It's like I had an internal checklist. Play dolls, style her hair, throw a girlie party, assemble furniture, roughhouse with her, hike a mountain, play laser tag, paint our nails, and get a little dirty. Now, I like to do all those things, but I put a lot of pressure on myself by thinking that I needed to make up for what she wanted. At one point, she also asked me to find someone quickly so she could have a Daddy. But she added, "If you don't find one, you're still enough mom."

The truth is, at times I didn't feel like I was enough. I was worried about filling all the possible voids. So in turn, I was overcompensating and not living in transparency, doing the best that I could. I wasn't grasping the fact that I simply needed to be myself, loving her the best I could. Sometimes kids will think the grass is greener, whether it's longing for a mother or father figure or simply wanting the neighbors' backyard trampoline. There will be moments of desires, questions, and confusion.

Even when a situation looks perfect, there are always moments of struggle and chaos. You're not alone in that. Though you have to bear a lot of weight on your own, you can provide a place of safety and peace that will carry your children through their journey. I was so afraid that my daughter would grow up to be angry and I wouldn't be enough. But I promise you, if you seek God in all you do, he somehow fills the spaces of your children's hearts and it's always more than enough. Through the love he gave me that I poured out into my daughter, I was able to take part in raising a very happy girl. It seemed like an impossible journey to me at one point, but to be on the other side is such a sweet feeling. To see how the Lord turned the messiest, most hopeless looking story into a testament of his goodness and faithfulness was and is transformative.

He can take the places where there seem to be huge pockets of emptiness and fill them. As I look back on my journey, I see how he used different people and situations to bring joy and completion to our lives. Through the love of a friend, the support of a church, or the generosity of our pastors, God came through. He never failed and was in every detail.

Beauty Mark

Trust in God and watch how he weaves your story into something beautiful. With God in the center, you will see that his plans are to heal our families and make us whole.

For I know the plans I have for you, declares the LORD, plans for welfare and not for evil, to give you a future and a hope.
JEREMIAH 29:11 ESV

Lord, I'm so grateful that you're more than enough. Fill the spaces in my heart and help me fully trust that you are in the details of my situation. Please give me wisdom and clarity on how to discuss sensitive topics with my children, and bring people into our path to be sources of encouragement and mentorship.

What is something you can let go of that makes you feel like you're not enough?

24

A Praying Mom

When I think back to what it was that helped sustain my positivity and optimism in the worst of times, it was prayer. Prayer is a constant thing in my life, so I never really say amen. I continually talk to God and thank him, ask a question, or beg him to bring change. Whether I was playing worship music on my iPod while on the elliptical, crying out for the Lord's guidance, or being in a face-plant plank position on my old apartment floor, I have asked God seemingly everything. He can handle all our questions and doubts no matter how big they are.

It can be frustrating when life gets serious and you feel like your prayers fall on deaf ears. That happened to me quite a bit, but I had to continue to trust that the Lord was working it out. (He always was—in ways that blew me away. Had some of my prayers been answered, I would be in serious trouble right now!) He knows our desires, but he also knows what's best for us, so he works everything out for good. Even when that's hard to believe or imagine, he truly does.

You may have some trouble hearing from God. I struggled with that quite a bit. Sometimes he answers with a peace in your spirit, a timely breakthrough, a phone call from a friend, or even a whisper to your soul. I've indeed had moments where I heard God speaking to me. Not in a loud, audible, booming voice, but a soft answer to my spirit, and I knew without a doubt the Lord had given me wisdom.

Throughout my journey as a single mom, I was faced with all kinds of moments when I needed God's answers. On one day in particular, I needed to know if I should file for a court hearing—a hearing that could protect my children and possibly answer some very big prayers. I remember so vividly being out on my balcony and hearing God so loudly in my soul saying that it was time. I went ahead and moved forward. Within days, I received a phone call that not only were we not going to have to go to court, but that my requests were fully granted.

Your answers may not come overnight, but when they come, it will be in a way that shakes your entire life to the core of its foundation. When God is in the middle, you will see your enemies hand over what was stolen. When you trust in the Lord, he will guide you into a life so full and so restored that you will look back with undeniable confirmation that he never left you or forsook you.

Do not grow weary in your prayers. Stay the course and know that in his time, God will make a way even when it seems impossible. There is a breakthrough in your story that will lead you into God's perfect, beautiful plan.

> *Let us not become weary in doing good, for at the proper time we will reap a harvest if we do not give up.*
>
> GALATIANS 6:9

God, I pray for a supernatural breakthrough in my story. Be near to me in my prayers and let me be so sensitive to your voice that when you say to move, I move.

What are some prayers you
have that need answers?

Journal

25

Are We Having Fun Yet?

Some days my two-year-old decides she wants to take matters into her own hands and remove a poop-filled diaper during naptime. How soon I catch her in the act determines exactly what I'm in for. At the same time, my teenager is upset and wants me to agree to let her see a movie that I don't agree with, so she throws somewhat of her own tantrum. Then my son, who is really quite easy but tends to forget things, is upset because he misplaced his iPhone and can't find it. Motherhood can be overwhelming, and this is one of the easier days.

When you have children, you have a full plate. Period. You never know what to expect, and you can easily let the buildup of frustrations and tension take you to places emotionally that you don't want to go. I've had a child around for my entire adult life. And now that I've started over again, I will surely be raising kids for a long time. I've never known what true independence was or how people can fly by the seat of their pants and wing it. They can run to a store and grab lunch, take a nap, or go out for dinner. What's that like? My life and my fun were wrapped around the schedules of my kids. I've never known any different.

I've had those kinds of days and have had some full-blown side punches when I'm in the middle of an already stressful situation. Some days you have to carry ten bags of groceries up the stairs, and one of the bags has a hole and your front yard has canned goods scattered on it. Then you burn your finger while cooking and drop a pan. The kids start screaming, and suddenly the emotions within you build and you want to burst into tears. These days are real! They happen and they don't have to get us off course.

There will be days when the joy feels like it's been sucked from the room by a vacuum cleaner. Laughing and being carefree seem like a thing of the past. Worries are near and relaxation feels miles away. I know when these days arose, it was sometimes hard to talk me out of the little hole I dug for myself. Why me? Why can't life be easier? Will I ever catch a break? Then maybe after a nap, a good cry, a full night's sleep, or a hug from my child, I'd slowly break through the sadness.

Be intentional with your joy. Yes, make time for joy. Life can get so wild that we forget to stop and laugh, do something funny with the kids, get our minds out of our own circumstances, and only live in the moment. Go on

YouTube and look up some karaoke tracks and sing along. Make some cookies and have a picnic. Play hide-and-seek in the dark. Being silly and lighthearted can bring a new energy into your home that can help everyone. It's important to create spaces that allow joy to come in and take over when doubts and exhaustion want be in the lead. Remember that the little things go so far.

Beauty
Mark

Create time to experience joy with your children. This will bring peace to them and also to you. Don't allow the insanity to come and take away what could end up being an amazing day.

For his anger lasts only a moment, but his favor lasts a lifetime; weeping may stay for the night, but rejoicing comes in the morning.

PSALM 30:5

Thank you, Lord, that you can restore joy in my life. Give me moments of rest and rejuvenation so I can have energy to be a source of happiness to my family. Give me creative ideas to infuse joy and peace into my home.

What is a fun activity you can do today
that would ease some of the pressure
and let light shine in?

26

Grace for the Moment

This morning I was watching the testimony of a woman who lost her husband to a sudden heart issue. She went on to marry a man who had lost his wife to cancer. They've come together in the most unimaginable way possible to bring hope to those grieving, salvation to those searching, and encouragement to those suffering. I sat in awe of her hope in such a tragic situation. They both had children they brought into the marriage and now have an incredibly moving testimony.

I found myself thinking, *How did they make it through? I could never go through that.* I can't imagine having hope and faith after losing my spouse. Then I find myself in a spiral of why bad things happen to good people. Why do God's followers ever have to suffer? Why was my life such a mess? How do people survive all this? Some questions have very clear answers and some don't. I know life is full of trials. If life were perfect, we'd already be in heaven.

Life can be confusing and just plain difficult. We don't have all the answers, and there are some things I can't wait to ask God about. We watched my brother suffer through a very rare cancer and lose his life. It still brings me to the point of confusion, but I know that God is still good. We can't fathom how people make it through certain trials with their faith intact, but God says he gives us peace that surpasses all understanding, so we surely can't understand it on this side of heaven.

I've had people tell me they can't believe I'm still standing and going after all these years. My trials were super hard, but they didn't seem as traumatic to me because in the midst of some very scary moments, I was still being held. I can clearly see that now. I was truly being walked through all of it by a God who is present in our suffering. I'd love for him to snap his fingers and make it all go away. Wouldn't that be nice? No pain, no suffering, no doubts, no hurting, no loneliness. Again, that would be called heaven. And he did promise us that. One day we will experience that freedom and all our suffering will be over.

Until then, we hold on to his promises. The promises that life was never meant to be easy but that he will be with us through each and every step of the way. We must be brave enough to hold on to that hope and not let go when our human minds can't comprehend the how and why. Through our trials, he is developing wisdom and perseverance in us and refining who we are as people. And when you can't understand, remember that his ways and thoughts are so much higher than ours. He knows your pain, your circumstances, and your questions. He has seen your tears and knows exactly what you need.

Beauty Mark

Know today that God's peace and strength can surpass any human understanding. Lean into him and his word, and he will uphold you in all your times of trouble. Through your faithfulness, he will continue to pour his love and blessings into your life.

> *And the peace of God, which surpasses all understanding, will guard your hearts and your minds in Christ Jesus.*
>
> PHILIPPIANS 4:7 ESV

Lord, I pray for peace in my heart. I pray that I trust you in every area of my life and that you continue to give me understanding of your greater plans. I ask you for continued strength in my trials and for renewed hope when I feel weak. Let your love overflow and be a strength I can't even comprehend.

In what area of your life do you need the
most grace right now? In what area
do you feel God upholding you?

Journal

27

Do You Feel What I Feel?

*L*ife can quickly become all about us. Depending on the age of our children, they may be too young to know what's going on or they may be old enough to be asking questions and wanting details. My story included betrayal, heartache, abuse, and abandonment. It was very easy to get wrapped up in how I felt and how things were personally affecting me. As much as I knew my child was suffering too, it was hard to cover all the bases.

If your story includes a messy divorce or a failed relationship, you've probably been through something that has hurt you. You have every right to take the time to grieve and grow. While you're going through or moving out of that season, it's so important to plug in to the needs of your children and ask questions about how they're feeling. I never wanted to look back with regret, but there were times when I was so wiped out that I would end up telling my daughter, "Let's talk later," a little too much.

Our children are an extension of our own heart. They hear, see, feel, and grieve in the same ways that we do. And when they don't fully understand the situation at hand, imagine the confusion they must feel. And if they have experienced the separation of their parents, their pain and heartache may mirror the things we're going through.

We have the ability to make life transitions so much better for our children if we allow them to walk through it with us. Of course they don't need all the details, but we can be thorough in our conversations, and open dialogue will make them feel safe and loved. Empathy is the ability to understand and share the feelings of another; that's what our children need. In fact, it's what our world needs. God can soften our heart toward our children to truly open up in ways that will allow them to flourish and feel peace even in a difficult time.

I think no matter how great of a job we do as a mommy, there are always ways we can learn to better connect with our children. My thirteen-year-old son recently told me, "Mom, you've set the standard high. I feel like I can tell you anything and you won't judge me." Cue the tears! I didn't always have this. A while back, I started being intentional with my interest and making those car rides home from school our full-on venting session. He tells me about his day, and I ask about his heart and if he's heard from his dad, how things are going, and what he needs. It's become our special time that I cherish.

I pray that God shows you ways to plug in to your children's needs and that you can have understanding and a listening ear for how life is treating them and what's going on with their fragile emotions. The more questions you ask and the more you show unwavering support, the more they'll come alive and open up to you.

Look for moments in the day to connect with your child's heart and emotions. An open dialogue will create freedom and beauty in your mother-child connection.

> *Start children off on the way they should go, and even when they are old they will not turn from it.*
>
> PROVERBS 22:6

God, help me turn my heart toward my children. Give me patience, wisdom, and understanding to empathize with their hurts and pains. Create a place of comfort and safety so that they feel my love and know I'm there for them.

How can you create moments
to connect with your child?

28

Spiritual Momentum

s single parents, we take on the role of spiritual leader in our household. To be in a place where we can hear from the Lord, and to be able to impart spiritual wisdom and guidance to our children, it must become a discipline for us. I personally have to be intentional about those moments because life can easily become noisy. Before you know it, so much is going on. To find that place of quiet and reprieve feels nearly impossible.

By investing time into reading the Word, praying, and meditating, not only do you become more sensitive to the voice of God, but you also feel a missing piece when you're not taking that time to connect. I find my time to connect once the kids are in bed. I'm able to really focus, pray, and read. I rotate anywhere from four to five books at a time—the Bible, a devotional, a study guide, or an encouraging biography. We can find encouragement and a spiritual pick-me-up in many things.

If you're having a night where focus and concentration are hard for you, just listen to worship music and pray. Try to unwind and just be in God's presence. Worship was always my great escape in the middle of a hard day when my mind wouldn't stop. Allow God into your day. The benefits you'll receive by taking time to be in his presence are so abundant. You can experience peace, wisdom, guidance, freedom, love, and fulfillment, and by having those moments of being spiritually refueled, you'll see that you're able to help set the pulse of your household. This is the absolute best gift you can give yourself and your family.

Beauty Mark

Take a moment every day to stop and be in the Lord's presence. Allow God into your day and he will renew your heart and mind.

> *Do not conform to the pattern of this world, but be transformed by the renewing of your mind. Then you will be able to test and approve what God's will is—his good, pleasing and perfect will.*
>
> ROMANS 12:2

God, help me find moments to recharge and connect. Speak to me through your Word and through being in your presence. I recognize my need for you in my heart and in my family. As I grow and mature spiritually, help me encourage closeness with you to my children and those around me.

What helps you recharge spiritually?
How can you make space in your life
for that every day?

Journal

29

Good Thing

In my early life, I often made decisions based on an emptiness I had in my heart. I grew up with a father who was wonderful at working hard to provide necessities we needed but didn't have an emotional connection to us. I wasn't asked questions, and he didn't take any interest in me. I just kind of floated through life without real human connection to a father figure.

This clouded my judgment when it came to choosing who I'd be in a relationship with because my standards were set to, "Oh, wow, he talks to me!" I didn't know how to gauge what my standards should be because I didn't recognize my value. This creeped into my love life, friendships, and business relationships. Because I didn't possess the ability to decipher good character, integrity, and honesty through my undying need for love and attention, I found myself in some scary situations.

You may be in a season of being single, you may be starting to make connections, or you may be just plain over it right now. Wherever you are in your life, set your internal worth meter to highly valuable. I can't tell you enough that, no matter what decisions you've made in your life and no matter how messy they may seem, you are extremely valuable and you should never settle for believing anything less. Had I not finally grasped the fact that I was worthy of love and respect, I would've never met my husband, who was (and is) totally awesome with my two kids—and he had never been married before.

You know the old saying that you attract to you what is within you? Well, it's true. Love yourself, value yourself, respect yourself, cherish yourself, and plug yourself in to God right now. This will decide what you'll connect to in your life. When you're being filled with his love, you'll clearly recognize the things that are so far away from that.

One of my spiritual moms, Dawn, told me several years ago in the middle of a desert of loneliness that I was someone's *good thing*. It was hard to believe when I couldn't see the good in my life. But she spoke words of life into my soul that reminded me of my worth. Then when I met my husband and we were getting serious, he wrote me a love note one day. On the front of the card he wrote, *To my good thing*. I called Dawn super excited because I knew it was a confirmation. The Bible says, "He who finds a wife, finds a good thing" (Proverbs 18:22).

You, wonderful you, are a very good thing. You, in all your glory, with your past, and in all the stages of confusion or difficulty in your life, are a very good thing. Lead your life in the knowledge that you're highly valuable. You are deserving of love, respect, time, and kindness from whomever you associate with. The creator of the universe is absolutely enamored with everything that you are. Not only does he know how many hairs are on your arm, but he also knows where you've been and has walked through even the darkest of moments with you. He values your existence, so you must boldly and confidently arise with the understanding that you are worth it.

Beauty
Mark

You are a very good thing. There is so much beauty in who you are. Remind yourself today that the creator of the universe thinks you're incredible and worth being treated with respect by everyone around you.

> *What marvelous love the Father has extended to us! Just look at it—we're called children of God! That's who we really are.*
> 1 JOHN 3:1 MSG

God, help me see how valuable I am. Let your love fill the spaces in my soul that need completion. Give me confidence to only allow myself to be treated the way you would want me to be treated—with love, honor, and respect.

What is something beautiful about you?

30

A True Miracle

To be honest, life could've brought me to a very different place. Between having a difficult childhood, being a teenage mom, and dealing with poverty and divorce, statistically, the fact that I'm writing to you today from a place of joy is a true miracle. Here's the deal. It's not because I'm more special than anyone else; it's because Jesus has been at the center.

You are a true miracle too. You have been called to do things in your life that you could never imagine. The amazing thing about Jesus is that he is really good at rewriting your script. By surrendering to him and allowing him to lead, you can be living out the most amazing, exciting, random, how-did-that-happen miracle.

By the age of twenty-six I thought my story was done. I had been there and done it all by that point—gotten divorced, had kids, and ended up broke, sad, and totally out of dreams. Then God grabbed ahold of my heart and found me in my sadness and shame. For the first time in my life, I started on a journey of finding who I am in him and seeing myself how he sees me.

The great thing about your story is that it's a wonderful opportunity to allow God a chance to blow your mind. I mean, run-around-the-church-and-holler type of stuff. There is a total plot twist that is going to happen that can give you more joy than you could ever imagine.

Do we really want a life that is led by us? I'll tell you what, the life that I was leading only took me through a hot, humid corn maze that I couldn't find my way out of. When I sat back and decided to allow God to take the lead, die to self and my own desires, and trust that, even when I didn't understand, he had my best interests at heart, things all started to align.

Who you are is a total miracle. Your life is a total miracle. Trust fully that God will take anything you're worried about or ashamed of and turn it around in such a way that you won't even recognize what your past looks like. He has dreams, visions, opportunities, and a testimony for you that will show all the people in your life what a wonderful and awesome God you serve.

Allow God to be your center, and trust that he's making your story into the greatest miracle.

> "In the end I will turn things around for the people. I'll give them a language undistorted, unpolluted, words to address God in worship and, united, to serve me with their shoulders to the wheel."
>
> ZEPHANIAH 3:9 MSG

Lord, make my life a miracle. I fully surrender to your will and trust that you can reignite my hope in the future. Give me an unbelievable story of grace so I can inspire others.

How is your life becoming a miracle?

Journal

31

It's How You Finish

ave you ever run a marathon? Okay, I for sure haven't. But if you have or have watched other people run such a race, you know that so much can happen from start to finish. People sprain ankles, and some get dehydrated or exhausted. Some may need help along the way while others get to the halfway point and get a resurgence of excitement and a second wind. It's an unpredictable experience that can leave you winded and ready for a nap.

But when I'm on YouTube and the music is going and I'm watching someone who is almost to the finish line, I always get teary-eyed. The runner sees that the end is ahead and, whether they're hobbling, running, limping, in a wheel-chair, or being carried, they're ready to cross over in victory. At that point, nothing else matters—not how many times they stopped, when they wanted to give up, or when they couldn't imagine ever racing through the final lap. All they can see is that they actually did it. They got through and finished well.

Life will be full of detours, distractions, and diversions. One day you have a resurgence of faith, and on another day you feel like you're too weak to finish what you started. This is the story for all of us. We're all running in this race together, and none of us are going to have totally smooth sailing.

I can tell you with certainty that you will not be upset that you didn't give up. Just like I never regret going to the gym (when it's over), you will not regret fighting through the uncertainties of your race and finishing strong. You have everything you need to get through this. I can't promise you won't have a few battle scars, but when you finally see the finish line, you'll soon forget the pain it took to get there.

Be strong. Be brave. Be courageous. Live your life with purpose and set your intentions on never giving up. The Bible says we will experience trials of many kinds but to let them do their work so we become mature and well-developed, not deficient in any way (James 1:2–4).

Life is not about the mistakes we've made, the detours we've taken, or the times we've done our own thing. It's not about the failures, the setbacks, the upsets, or the frustrations. You must continue to stand. You must continue to run. You must continue to believe. And you must never, ever give up.

Live well, trust in the Lord with all your heart, and finish strong.

See the beauty and purpose in your life. Believe that you're strong and courageous and that Jesus is carrying you through to the finish line in your trial.

> I have fought a good fight, I have finished my course, I have kept the faith.
>
> 2 TIMOTHY 4:7 KJV

Lord, help me never give up. Let me see that even through the trials, you are setting me up to finish strong and with courage. Be near to me and constantly remind me that I am not alone.

What are two things that you can do consistently that will help you finish strong?

Journal

Bible Promises for Single Moms

Children

Children are a gift from the LORD; they are a reward from
him.

PSALM 127:3 NLT

I have no greater joy than to hear that my children are
walking the in the truth.

3 JOHN 1:4

"Whoever receives one little child like this in My name
receives Me. …Take heed that you do not despise one of
these little ones, for I say to you that in heaven their angels
always see the face of My Father who is in heaven."

MATTHEW 18:5, 10 NKJV

Comfort

"I will comfort you there in Jerusalem as a mother comforts her child."

ISAIAH 66:13 NLT

Praise be to the God and Father of our Lord Jesus Christ, the Father of compassion and the God of all comfort.

2 CORINTHIANS 1:3

"I have seen what they do,
but I will heal them anyway!
I will lead them.
I will comfort those who mourn."

ISAIAH 57:18 NLT

Encouragement

The humble will see their God at work and be glad.
Let all who seek God's help be encouraged.

PSALM 69:32 NLT

Since we first heard about you, we've kept you always in
our prayers that you would receive the perfect knowledge
of God's pleasure over your lives, making you reservoirs
of every kind of wisdom and spiritual understanding. We
pray that you would walk in the ways of true righteousness,
pleasing God in every good thing you do. Then you'll
become fruit-bearing branches, yielding to his life, and
maturing in the rich experience of knowing God in his
fullness!

COLOSSIANS 1:9–10 TPT

Let everything you say be good and helpful, so that your
words will be an encouragement to those who hear them.

EPHESIANS 4:29 NLT

Faith

Without faith it is impossible to please God, because anyone who comes to him must believe that he exists and that he rewards those who earnestly seek him.

HEBREWS 11:6

Faith comes by hearing, and hearing by the word of God.

ROMANS 10:17 NKJV

Faith is confidence in what we hope for and assurance about what we do not see.

HEBREWS 11:1

Finances

Don't love money; be satisfied with what you have.
For God has said, "I will never fail you. I will never abandon you."

HEBREWS 13:5 NLT

My God will meet all your needs according to the riches of his glory in Christ Jesus.

PHILIPPIANS 4:19

As for the rich in this present age, charge them not to be haughty, nor to set their hopes on the uncertainty of riches, but on God, who richly provides us with everything to enjoy.

1 TIMOTHY 6:17 ESV

Grace

God saved you by his grace when you believed. And you can't take credit for this; it is a gift from God. Salvation is not a reward for the good things we have done, so none of us can boast about it.

EPHESIANS 2:8–9 NLT

Sin is no longer your master, for you no longer live under the requirements of the law. Instead, you live under the freedom of God's grace.

ROMANS 6:14 NLT

His unforgettable works of surpassing wonder reveal his grace and tender mercy.

PSALM 111:4 TPT

Health

A cheerful heart is good medicine.

PROVERBS 17:22

"Daughter, because you dared to believe, your faith has healed you. Go with peace in your heart, and be free from your suffering!"

MARK 5:34 TPT

Trust the LORD with all your heart,
and don't depend on your own understanding.
Remember the LORD in all you do,
and he will give you success.
Don't depend on your own wisdom.
Respect the LORD and refuse to do wrong.
Then your body will be healthy,
and your bones will be strong.

PROVERBS 3:5–8 NCV

Hope

He lifts the poor from the dust
and the needy from the garbage dump.
He sets them among princes,
placing them in seats of honor.
For all the earth is the LORD's,
and he has set the whole world in order.

1 SAMUEL 2:8 NLT

May the God of hope fill you with all joy and peace as you
trust in him, so that you may overflow with hope by the
power of the Holy Spirit.

ROMANS 15:13

Blessed be the God and Father of our Lord Jesus Christ!
According to his great mercy, he has caused us to be born
again to a living hope through the resurrection of Jesus
Christ.

1 PETER 1:3 ESV

Joy

So be truly glad. There is wonderful joy ahead, even though you must endure many trials for a little while. … You love him even though you have never seen him. Though you do not see him now, you trust him; and you rejoice with a glorious, inexpressible joy.

1 PETER 1:6, 8 NLT

"Until now you have not asked for anything in my name. Ask and you will receive, and your joy will be complete."

JOHN 16:24

Light shines on the righteous and joy on the upright in heart.

PSALM 97:11 NIV

Love

Don't just pretend to love others. Really love them. Hate what is wrong. Hold tightly to what is good. Love each other with genuine affection, and take delight in honoring each other.

ROMANS 12:9–10 NLT

These things last forever—faith, hope, and love—and the greatest of these is love.

1 CORINTHIANS 13:13 NLT

Above all, love each other deeply, because love covers over a multitude of sins.

1 PETER 4:8

We know what real love is because Jesus gave up his life for us. So we also ought to give up our lives for our brothers and sisters.

1 JOHN 3:16 NLT

Patience

They who wait for the LORD
shall renew their strength;
they shall mount up with wings like eagles;
they shall run and not be weary;
they shall walk and not faint.

ISAIAH 40:31 ESV

Make me truly happy by agreeing wholeheartedly with each
other, loving one another, and working together with one
mind and purpose.

PHILIPPIANS 2:2 NLT

Escort me along the way;
take me by the hand and teach me.
For you are the God of my increasing salvation;
I have wrapped my heart into yours!

PSALM 25:5 TPT

Peace

The LORD will give strength to His people;
the LORD will bless His people with peace.

PSALM 29:11 NKJV

Let the peace of Christ rule in your hearts, since as
members of one body you were called to peace. And be
thankful.

COLOSSIANS 3:15

"I have told you all this so that you may have peace in me.
Here on earth you will have many trials and sorrows. But
take heart, because I have overcome the world."

JOHN 16:33 NLT

Now may the Lord of peace himself give you peace at all
times and in every way. The Lord be with all of you.

2 THESSALONIANS 3:16

Prayer

Pray about everything. Tell God what you need, and thank him for all he has done.

PHILIPPIANS 4:6 NLT

Confess your sins to each other and pray for each other so that you may be healed. The prayer of a righteous person is powerful and effective.

JAMES 5:16

"Ask and it will be given to you; seek and you will find; knock and the door will be opened to you. For everyone who asks receives; the one who seeks finds; and to the one who knocks, the door will be opened."

MATTHEW 7:7–8

Rest

Those who live in the shelter of the Most High
will find rest in the shadow of the Almighty.

PSALM 91:1 NLT

This is what the LORD says:
"Stand at the crossroads and look;
ask for the ancient paths,
ask where the good way is, and walk in it,
and you will find rest for your souls."

JEREMIAH 6:16

God's promise of entering his rest still stands, so we ought
to tremble with fear that some of you might fail to experience it.

HEBREWS 4:1 NLT

Strength

In your strength I can crush an army;
with my God I can scale any wall.

2 SAMUEL 22:30 NLT

The LORD gives strength to his people.

PSALM 29:11

You empower me for victory
with your wrap-around presence.
Your power within makes me strong to subdue,
and by stooping down in gentleness
you strengthened me and made me great!

PSALM 18:35 TPT

My flesh and my heart fail;
But God is the strength of my heart
and my portion forever.

PSALM 73:26 NKJV

About the Author

ikki Leonti Edgar was raised singing in church with her family, and her love of music was birthed through hearing the sounds of gospel choirs. She experienced the loss of a brother through cancer at a very young age, but she was inspired by her family's continuous faith through that tragedy.

Nikki had a successful Christian music career with number-one songs and charting album sales, but it wasn't enough to fill the emptiness inside her. She found herself alone with two children by the time she was twenty-four years old, and soon moved to California and began to create a business for herself, all while being a single mom for nearly a decade. Throughout her time in California, she wrote music for television and film that spanned all genres. Her credits include multiple Disney and Dreamworks movies, lending vocals to over two hundred songs on Fox's hit show *Glee*, as well as backing vocals for albums and live shows for artists such as Rod Stewart, Carrie Underwood, Katy Perry,

Demi Lovato, CeeLo Green, Amy Grant, Selena Gomez, Faith Hill, Josh Groban, Pharrell Williams, Kirk Franklin, and many others. She has written songs for various artists, including Jessie J, Robin Thicke, Candice Glover, Rebecca Ferguson, Olivia Holt, and Dove Cameron. During her years of being single, she found strength in God and an incredible peace with being alone.

At the end of 2013, Nikki was given God's greatest gift through the love of the wonderful man who is now her husband, Ryan Edgar. He adopted her older daughter and has been very supportive of Nikki. They just completed their run on NBC's hit show *America's Got Talent* and made it to the semifinals. The family is actively involved in their church through worship arts and are pursuing various avenues of music through writing and live shows. They look forward to the adventure ahead and how God can use their stories to ignite hope in others.

To learn more about Nikki, visit NikkiEdgar.com.